Noah's Ark

Written by Sasha Morton
Illustrated by Alfredo Belli

Long before the time of Jesus, there lived a man named Noah.
He and his family lived in a way that made God very happy.

But other people in the world
were fighting, stealing and arguing.
This made God very sad.

One day, God spoke to Noah. He wanted to put an end to the evil that was ruining the world and he needed Noah's help.

He asked Noah and his family to collect a pair of animals
from every species on Earth. Then he asked Noah
to build an enormous ark, on which they would all fit.
God was going to send a flood to wash away all the evil.

Noah and his family set
to work straight away.

They gathered two of
every animal and kept
them safe until their new
home was ready.

Next, they began to build the enormous ark. They chopped, sawed and hammered until after a great deal of hard work…

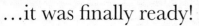

…it was finally ready!
　　As soon as the ark was complete, the sky grew dark,
　　　　the air grew still, the birds stopped twittering in the trees…

…and a heavy rain began.

8

Noah and his family
led the animals aboard
the ark and they waited.

The rain fell and fell and soon
the ark rose up and began to float!

Huge drops fell from the sky until everything on the Earth was covered with water, even the mountain tops.

Everything would be washed away by the great flood.

Life on the ark was hard, especially with so
many animals to feed and keep clean.

Noah's family were tired and worried.
"Will the rain ever stop, Noah?" asked his wife.
"It is all part of God's plan," said Noah, as he
looked out at the rising seas.

But as the days passed, they wondered if
they would ever leave the ark again.

13

It rained for forty days and forty nights, and then as suddenly as it had started, the rain stopped!

The sun began to shine through the clouds and a swift wind blew.

As they drifted across the
endless ocean, Noah saw
something above the water…

…it was land!

The ark drifted over to the top of
the mountain. Then Noah quickly released a
dove to see if it would find any more dry land.

They watched as the dove flew up
and over the horizon, then they waited.

But the dove soon flew back,
for there was nowhere for it to land.

After a week, Noah sent
the dove out once more.

They watched the bird fly up and away, and before long the dove came back carrying an olive branch!

It must have found a tree above the water!

The dove dropped the branch, then it flew from the ark and did not come back. Noah realised the land was dry enough to live on again. It was time for their new lives to begin at last.

After many days at sea, the great flood
was over. Noah stepped onto dry land and led
his family and all the animals into a new world.

Noah and his family knelt down
and thanked God for saving them.
They promised to create a peaceful new
world, which would make God happy.

To reward him, God made Noah a promise.

He said, "I will never again send a flood to destroy the world. Instead, every time it rains, I will send a symbol to remind all living creatures on Earth that I will always keep them safe."

And to this day, God is true to his word.
For whenever sun and rain appear in the sky together,
a rainbow does indeed shine over the world.

An Hachette UK Company
www.hachette.co.uk

First published in Great Britain in 2013 by TickTock,
an imprint of Octopus Publishing Group Ltd,
Endeavour House,
189 Shaftesbury Avenue,
London WC2H 8JY.

www.octopusbooks.co.uk

lSBN 978 1 84898 816 3

A CIP record of this book is available from the British Library

Printed and bound in China

1 3 5 7 10 8 6 4 2

With thanks to: Jana Burson

Series Editor: Lucy Cuthew   Design: Advocate Art
Publisher: Tim Cook   Managing Editor: Karen Rigden
Production: Lucy Carter